Margie

5 LITTLE CRITTERS

9 ELIE ELEPHANT

13 ROBBY RACCOON

14 SWEET SUZY

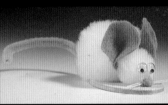

19 STRIPES

D1614206

10 DOLLY DRAGON

6 SALLY SQUIRREL

15 LIL' COUNTRY GIRL

20 MOLLY MOUSE

11 BANANA MONKEY

7 FREDDY FROGGY

16 WALLY WALRUS

21 PETER POLARCONE

12 TIMMY TROLL

17 POM-POM PETS

8 KATY KOALA

22 PENNY PANDA

2 CONTENTS

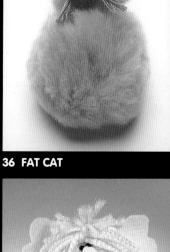
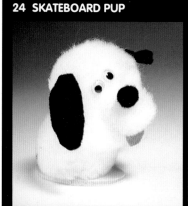

CONTENTS 3

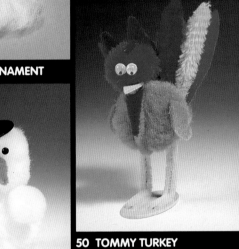

CONTENTS

4

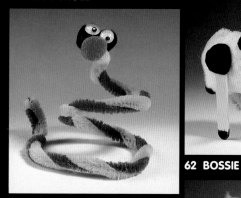

Little Critters

Sally Squirrel

Freddy Froggy

Katy Koala

Elie Elephant

Dolly Dragon

Banana Monkey

Timmy Troll

Robby Raccoon

Sweet Suzy

Lil' Country Girl

1. Glue eyes and nose in place on face.

2. Cut ears from tan felt and glue in place.

CUT 2 EARS

3. Glue head to body.

4. Cut 2 pieces of tan chenille 3/4" long and glue in place for arms. Glue 1/4" brown pom-pom in "paws".

5. Glue assembled head and body on to round wood shape.

6. Cut one section of brown bump chenille, curl and glue in place as tail.

7. Cut 6 short pieces of cat whiskers 1/2" to 3/4" and glue under nose.

MATERIALS

2 - 1" TAN POM-POMS (HEAD AND BODY)

1 -1/4" BROWN POM-POM (NUT)

2 - 7mm WIGGLE EYES

1 - 3mm BLACK BEAD (NOSE)

TAN CHENILLE

BURNT ORANGE BUMP CHENILLE

TAN FELT

CAT WHISKERS

1 - 1/4" ROUND WOOD SHAPE (BASE)

1. Glue wiggle eyes to 1/4" light green pom-poms. Glue the pom-poms together. Then glue assembled eyes on top of one of the dark green 1" pom-poms.

2. Cut mouth from light green felt. Fold in half and glue top half to the bottom of the head and the bottom half to the top of the body. Cut tongue from dark pink felt and glue to back of mouth.

3. Cut 2 pieces of dark green chenille 2 1/4" long and fold in half for legs.

4. Cut flippers from dark green felt and lily pad from light green felt.

5. Glue flippers to center of lily pad and assembled frog on top of flippers. Add legs and glue completed piece to oval wood shape base.

MATERIALS

2 - 1" GREEN POM-POMS (HEAD & BODY)

2 - 1/4" LIGHT GREEN POM-POMS (BEHIND EYES)

2 - 5MM WIGGLE EWES

LIGHT GREEN, DARK GREEN, DARK PINK FELT

DARK GREEN CHENILLE

2" OVAL WOOD SHAPE (BASE)

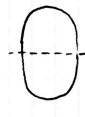

MOUTH

TONGUE

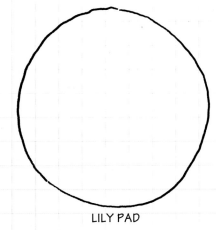

LILY PAD

FLIPPERS

MOUTH IS CREATED BY GLUING THE FOLDED FELT TO THE 2 POM-POMS AS SHOWN

1. Cut nose from black felt and glue on center of head. Glue eyes on either side of nose.

2. Cut ears from burnt orange felt and glue in place on head.

3. Glue the head to the body and the assembled figure to the round wood shape for support.

4. Add the tail.

MATERIALS

2 - 1" TAN POM-POMS (HEAD & BODY)

1 - 1/4" TAN POM-POM (TAIL)

2 - 3mm BLACK BEADS (EYES)

BURNT ORANGE AND BLACK FELT

1 - 1 1/2" ROUND WOOD SHAPE

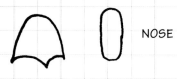

NOSE

CUT 2 EARS

1. Cut ears from lavender felt and glue to head as shown.

2. Add trunk and eyes.

3. Glue body to head and add tail.

4. Cut medium blue chenille into 4 pieces 1" long and glue to body for legs.

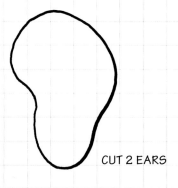

CUT 2 EARS

MATERIALS

2 - 1" PURPLE POM-POMS (HEAD & BODY)

2 - 6mm WIGGLE EYES

LAVENDER FELT (EARS)

PURPLE BUMP CHENILLE (TRUNK & TAIL)

MEDIUM BLUE CHENILLE (LEGS)

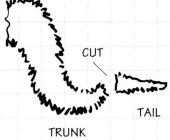

CUT

TAIL

TRUNK

MATERIALS

3 - 1" DARK GREEN POM-POMS

1 - 1" LIGHT GREEN POM-POMS

2 - 1/4" LIGHT GREEN POM-POMS (BEHIND EYES)

2 - 5mm PINK POM-POMS (TEETH)

2 - 3mm BLACK BEADS (NOSE)

2 - 6 mm WIGGLE EYES

DARK GREEN CHENILLE

DARK GREEN AND HOT PINK FELT

2" OVAL WOOD SHAPE (BASE)

1. Glue wiggle eyes to 1/4" light green pom-poms.

2. Cut mouth from hot green felt, fold in half . Glue top half to one dark green pom-pom and bottom half to second dark green pom-pom as shown. Glue the pom-poms together at the back like a hinge.

3. Glue assembled eyes to top of head. Glue black beads in place for nostrils.

4. Glue a dark green and light green pom-pom together and attach to back of lower head as shown in drawing.

5. Cut about 3" of green chenille and bend to shape the tail. Glue in place.

6. Cut dragon's mane from green felt and glue on head.

7. Glue "teeth" into mouth. Glue assembled model to oval wood shape.

MOUTH

MANE

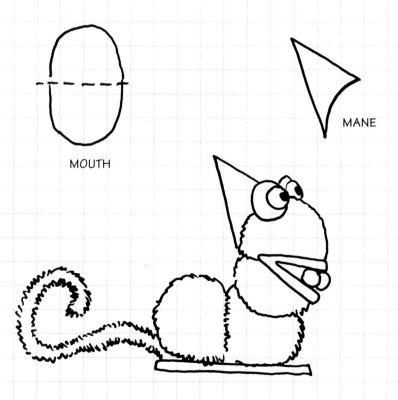

1. Trim some of the fuzz off the tan pom-pom to make it flatter. Glue the nose to the top of it. Glue the assembled pieces to the lower half of the head.

2. Cut face from tan felt and glue on head above face. Glue eyes as shown.

3. Cut ears from tan felt and glue to side of head. Glue completed head to body.

4. Make arms, feet and tail from brown chenille and glue to body. The left arm is a little longer than the right arm to make a hand to wrap around the banana.

5. Glue body to square wood shape.

6. Make banana from yellow chenille, wrap in peel cut from felt and glue to hand.

7. The smile is achieved by trimming the 1/2" tan pom-pom slightly more to create the effect of a smiling upper lip.

MATERIALS

1 - 1" BROWN POM-POM (HEAD)
1 - 3/4" BROWN POM-POM (BODY)
1 - 1/2" TAN POM-POM
1 - 3mm BLACK BEAD (NOSE)
2 - 5mm WIGGLE EYES
TAN AND YELLOW-ORANGE FELT
BROWN AND YELLOW CHENILLE
1 - 1 7/8" SQUARE WOOD SHAPE

FACE

CUT 2 EARS

BANANA PEEL

1. Glue body and head together.

2. Add eyes and nose.

3. Cut ears, hands and feet from pink felt and glue on body as shown.

4. Cut a bunch of wool doll hair a little bigger than shown in the drawing. Pinch the bottom together and glue to top of head. Hold in place until dry. You can trim it to shape after it is in place.

FEET

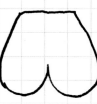

CUT 2 EARS

CUT 2 HANDS

MATERIALS

2 - 1" PINK POM-POMS (HEAD & BODY)

1 - 5 mm PINK POM-POM (NOSE)

2 - 5mm WIGGLE EYES

PINK FELT

WHITE WOOL DOLL HAIR

CUT APPROXIMATELY THIS
MUCH WHITE WOOL DOLL HAIR

1. Cut mask from black felt and glue to light blue pom-pom.

2. Glue on black beads for eyes and nose.

3. Cut outer and inner ears from light blue and black felt. Glue the black on the blue and then to the head in place.

4. Glue head to body and then glue body to round wood shape.

5. Cut whiskers to about 1/2" length and glue under nose.

6. Add a 1" piece of bump chenille for tail.

MATERIALS

1 - 1" BLACK POM-POM (BODY)

1 - 1" LIGHT BLUE POM-POM (BODY)

3 - 3mm BLACK BEADS (NOSE & EYES)

BLACK BUMP CHENILLE

LIGHT BLUE AND BLACK FELT

CAT WHISKERS

1 3/4" ROUND WOOD SHAPE

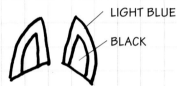

LIGHT BLUE

BLACK

MASK

MASK
CURVES
AROUND
HEAD

1. Glue eyes and nose to 1" black pom-pom.

2. Glue head to body.

3. Cut ears from black felt and glue to head.

CUT 2 EARS

4. Make tail and white stripe from sections of black and white bump chenille. The white mane on the top of head is a short section of white chenille.

5. Paint wood base black and attach body.

6. Add tail and white stripe.

MATERIALS

2 -1" BLACK POM-POMS (HEAD & BODY)

1 - 5mm PINK POM-POM (NOSE)

2 - 5mm WIGGLE EYES

CAT WHISKERS

BLACK FELT (EARS)

BLACK AND WHITE BUMP CHENILLE

1 - 1 1/4" ROUND WOOD SHAPE

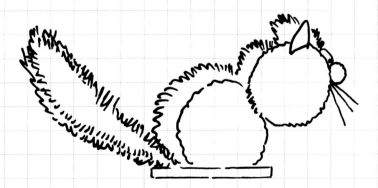

1. Glue nose and eyes to head.

2. Glue head to body.

3. Cut approximately 20 strands 3 1/2" of embroidery floss. The easiest way to do this is to cut across the whole top of the packaged floss as shown.

4. Glue hair to top of head.

5. Glue assembled model to wood shape and glue hat in place.

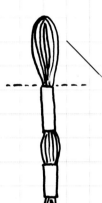

SLIDE DOWN THE LARGE WRAPPER AND CUT OFF EVERY THING ABOVE FOR HAIR

MATERIALS

2 - 1" PURPLE POM-POMS (HEAD & BODY)

1 - 1/4" GREEN POM-POM

2 - 6mm WIGGLE EYES

HOT PINK EMBROIDERY FLOSS

STRAW HAT

1 - 1 1/8" ROUND WOOD SHAPE

1. Glue eyes and both 1/4" brown pom-poms to head.

2. Glue head to body and add the tail.

3. Cut flippers from burnt orange felt and glue to tail.

4. Glue assembly to oval wood shape.

5. Cut 2 pieces of white chenille to 1 1/8" and glue in place on face.

MATERIALS

1 - 1" BROWN POM-POM (BODY)

2 - 3/4" BROWN POM-POMS (HEAD & TAIL)

2 - 1/4" BROWN POM-POMS

2 - 6mm WIGGLE EYES

WHITE CHENILLE (TUSKS)

BURNT ORANGE FELT (FLIPPERS)

1 - 1 1/2" OVAL WOOD SHAPE

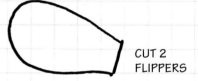

CUT 2 FLIPPERS

Pompom Pets

1. Glue together the 2 black cheeks.

2. Glue red and pink pom-poms on cheeks for nose and mouth.

3. Glue assembled pieces to head and eyes as shown.

4. Cut ears from black felt and glue to head. Glue assembled head to body.

 CUT 2 EARS

5. Make a 3/4" ball of yarn and glue it together.

6. Glue assembled cat to round wood shape and wrap with yarn until it looks tangled enough to suit you. Glue whwerver necessary to hold in place.

7. Cut a section of black bump chenille for tail and glue.

8. Cut about 12 pieces of cat whiskers 3/4" long and glue in place around nose.

MATERIALS

1 - 1 1/2" BLACK POM-POM (BODY)

1 - 1" BLACK POM-POM (HEAD)

2 - 1/2" BLACK POM-POMS (CHEEKS)

1 - 1/4" RED POM-POM (NOSE)

1 - 3mm PINK POM-POM (MOUTH)

2 - 5mm WIGGLE EYES

BLACK BUMP CHENILLE (TAIL)

CAT WHISKERS

BLACK FELT

THICK MAUVE YARN

1 3/4" ROUND WOOD SHAPE

1. Glue oval wood shapes to wooden spoon as shown in drawing. Paint with pink and orange stripes.

2. Glue the cheeks together and glue the nose on top at center. Glue assembled nose and cheeks to top of spoon as shown.

3. Add eyes and bow (make your own bow or buy one pre-made).

4. Cut a section of pink bump chenille and glue in place on back.

5. Glue the assembled cat to the base and support with a small wood shape glued in place as a prop.

6. Cut 6 pieces of cat whiskers 1" long and glue under nose.

MATERIALS

2 - 1/2" PINK POM-POMS (CHEEKS)

1 - 1/4" RED POM-POM (NOSE)

2 - 5mm WIGGLE EYES

CAT WHISKERS

RED BOW

WOODEN SPOON

6 OVAL POINTED WOOD SHAPES (LARGE, MEDIUM, SMALL)

PINK BUMP CHENILLE (TAIL)

2 1/4" OVAL WOOD SHAPE (BASE)

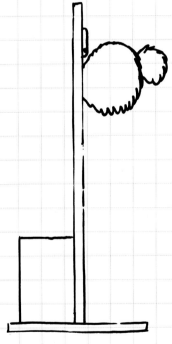

PROP UP CAT WITH A
SMALL PIECE OF WOOD
GLUED IN BACK

MATERIALS

1 - 1 1/2" WHITE POM-POM (BODY)

1 - 3/4" WHITE POM-POM (HEAD)

2 - 6mm WIGGLE EYES

1 - 5mm PINK POM-POM (NOSE)

CAT WHISKERS

PINK CHENILLE (TAIL)

MEDIUM PINK FELT (EARS)

2 1/4" OVAL WOOD SHAPE

1. Glue head, body and nose in place on oval base.

2. Cut ears from pink felt and glue ends as shown in drawing. Attach to head.

3. Cut 4" pink chenille, curl slightly and glue in place for tail.

4. Add whiskers.

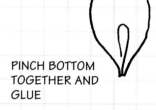

CUT 2 EARS

PINCH BOTTOM
TOGETHER AND
GLUE

1. Trim some of the fuzz off of one of the large white pom-poms to make a slightly smaller shape for the head,

2. Glue 3/4" white nose to head. Add black bead to tip of nose.

3. Glue eyes and ears in position on head.

4. Glue head to body.

5. Make one arm and tail from 3/4" pom-pom and glue to body.

6. Glue assembled bear to oval wood shape.

7. Cut cone from yellow-ochre felt. Curl and glue at seam. Glue cone to bear's side. Add the 4 colored pom-poms (any flavor you like).

MATERIALS

2 - 1 1/2" WHITE POM-POMS (HEAD & BODY)

3 - 3/4" WHITE POM-POMS (ARM, NOSE & TAIL)

2 - 1/4" WHITE POM-POMS (EARS)

2 - 7mm WIGGLE EYES

1 - 3mm BLACK BEAD (NOSE)

4 - 4/3" POM-POMS - GREEN, YELLOW, PINK, PURPLE (ICE CREAM)

YELLOW-OCHRE FELT (CONE)

WHITE CHENILLE (ARMS)

2" OVAL WOOD SHAPE (BASE)

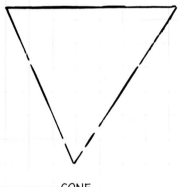

CONE

GLUE SEAM

1. Glue nose (1/2" black pom-pom) to center of head.

2. Cut eyes and mouth from black felt and glue around nose. Cut ears and glue to head as shown.

3. Trim the black 2" pom-pom by cutting off much of the fur to make a flattened shape for the upper body. Glue that trimmed shape to the lower body. Glue the completed head to the upper body.

4. The arms and legs are also trimmed black pom-poms. Cut off enough fur to male long cylindrical shapes. Glue to body as shown.

5. Cut 3 pieces 3 1/2" long white chenille and glue the 3 colored balloons to the tops. Glue the balloons and their "strings" to the right arm of the panda and then glue one 1/2" black pom-pom over the strings to look like a paw.

6. Add the tail.

MATERIALS

3 - 3/4" POM-POMS, RED, GREEN & DARK BLUE (BALLOONS)

1 - 2" WHITE POM-POM (LOWER BODY)

1 - 2" BLACK POM-POM (UPPER BODY)

1 - 1 1/2" WHITE POM-POM (HEAD)

4 - 1" BLACK POM-POMS (ARMS & LEGS)

2 - 1/2" BLACK POM-POMS (PAW & NOSE)

1 - 1/4 " BLACK POM-POM (TAIL)

BLACK FELT

WHITE CHENILLE

CUT 2 EYES

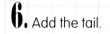

MOUTH

CUT 2 EARS

1. Create nose, lips and chin from 1/2" tan pom-poms, pink and black felt as shown in drawing. To make the chin, trim some of the fur off of one of the 1/2" pom-poms. Glue assembly to head.

2. Glue eyes over nose.

3. Cut ears from tan felt and glue to head.

4. Glue head to body.

5. Glue assembled body to base.

6. Add feet, paws and tail.

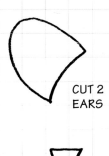

CUT 2
EARS

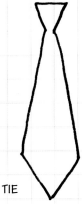

TIE

MATERIALS

2 - 2" TAN POM POMS (HEAD & BODY)

3 - 3/4" TAN POM-POMS (NOSE & FEET)

4 - 1/2" TAN POM-POMS (PAWS, TAIL & CHIN)

2 - 7mm WIGGLE EYES

HOT PINK, TAN AND BLACK FELT

2 1/4" OVAL WOOD SHAPE

NOSE
LIPS
CHIN

LIPS

NOSE

1. Glue together 2 pink 1/2" pom-poms and center red pom-pom on top.

2. Glue assembly to head and add eyes.

3. Glue head to body and add paws as shown.

4. Cut tongue from dark pink felt and ears from lavender felt and glue in place.

5. Glue assembled body to wooden spoon. Glue the 2 wooden spools to the under side of the spoon to make wheels.

MATERIALS

1 - 2" PINK POM-POM (HEAD)

1 - 1 1/2" PINK POM-POM (BODY)

4 - 1/2" PINK POM-POMS (NOSE & PAWS)

1 - 1/4" RED POM-POM (NOSE)

2 - 7mm WIGGLE EYES

LAVENDER BUMP CHENILLE

LAVENDER AND DARK PINK FELT

WOODEN SPOON

2 WOODEN SPOOLS

TONGUE

CUT 2
EARS

1. Glue one 1/4" black pom-pom to the 3/4" white pom-pom to make nose and snout. Glue to head.

2. Glue eyes in place above nose.

3. Cut ears from black felt and tongue from dark pink felt and glue to head as shown.

4. Glue tail to back.

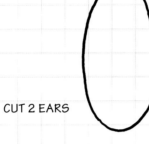

CUT 2 EARS

TONGUE

MATERIALS

1 - 2" WHITE POM-POM (HEAD)

1 - 1 1/2" WHITE POM-POM (BODY)

1 - 3/4" WHITE POM-POM

2 - 1/4" BLACK POM-POMS (NOSE & TAIL)

2 - 7mm WIGGLE EYES

BLACK FELT (EARS)

DARK PINK FELT (TONGUE)

2 1/4" OVAL WOOD SHAPE (BASE)

MATERIALS

1 - 2" PINK POM-POM (BODY)

1 - 1 1/2" PINK POM-POM (HEAD)

2 - 3/4" PINK POM-POMS (SNOUT)

1 - 1/4" PINK POM-POM (CHIN)

1 - 1/4" RED POM-POM (NOSE)

2 - 5mm WIGGLE EYES

CAT WHISKERS

DARK PINK FELT (EARS)

YELLOW-ORANGE FELT (CAP)

ORANGE BUMP CHENILLE (TAIL)

1 3/4" ROUND WOOD SHAPE (BASE)

1. Glue together 2 - 3/4" pink pom-poms, 1 - 1/4" pink pom-pom and 1 - 1/4" red pom-pom to make nose, snout and mouth as shown.

2. Glue assembly to head.

CUT 2 EARS

3. Cut ears from dark pink felt and glue to head. Glue eyes in place.

4. Glue assembled head to body and glue body to base.

5. Cut one section of orange bump chenille and glue in place for tail.

6. Cut whiskers and glue under nose.

7. Cut cap from yellow-orange felt, glue together and glue to head.

CAP

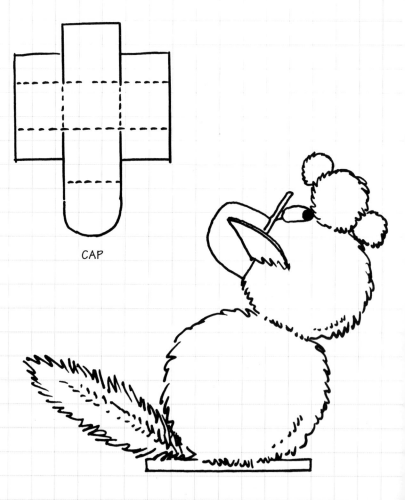

1. Glue nose to snout and snout to head.

2. Glue eyes in place over snout.

3. Cut tongue from dark pink felt and glue in place under nose.

4. Glue head to body and legs in place as shown.

5. Cut ears from gray felt and glue on head.

6. Paint supper dish any bright color you like.

MATERIALS

2 - 1 1/2" WHITE POM-POMS (HEAD & BODY)

5 - 3/4" WHITE POM-POMS (LEGS & SNOUT)

1 - 5mm PINK POM-POM (NOSE)

1 - 1/4" WHITE POM-POM (TAIL)

2 - 6mm WIGGLE EYES

GRAY FELT (EARS)

DARK PINK FELT (TONGUE)

WOOD DOLL STAND (SUPPER DISH)

TONGUE

CUT 2
EARS

Wearables

Teddy Pin

Three Faces
Hairpin

Wish 'n' wears

Teddy Hairbow

Bunny pin

1. Glue the snout to the head slightly below center.

2. Glue the nose to the center of the snout.

3. Glue the eyes in place over the snout.

CUT 2
EARS

4. Cut ears from burnt-orange felt and glue in place.

5. Glue the completed face to the round wood base.

6. Cut 2 pieces of calico ribbon about 5/8" x 3" and glue to back of wood shape as shown.

7. Glue jewelry pin back over ribbons.

MATERIALS

1 - 1 1/2" TAN POM-POM (HEAD)

1 - 1/2" TAN POM-POM (SNOUT)

2 - 5mm WIGGLE EYES

1 - 3mm BLACK BEAD (NOSE)

1 - 1" JEWELRY PIN BACK

BURNT-ORANGE FELT (EARS)

CALICO RIBBON

1 1/4" ROUND WOOD SHAPE (BASE)

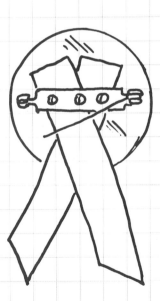

MATERIALS

KITTY

1 - 1" PINK POM-POM (HEAD)

2 - 1/4" PINK POM-POMS (SNOUT)

2 - 3mm BLACK BEADS (EYES)

PINK FELT (EARS)

CAT WHISKERS

TEDDY

1 - 1" TAN POM-POM (HEAD)

1 - 1/2" TAN POM-POM (SNOUT)

2 - 1/4" TAN POM-POMS (EARS)

3 - 3mm BLACK BEADS (EYES & NOSE)

BUNNY

1 - 1" LIGHT BLUE POM-POM (HEAD)

2 - 1/4" LIGHT BLUE POM-POMS (SNOUT)

1 - 3mm PINK POM-POM 9NOSE)

2- 3mm BLACK BEADS (EYES)

LIGHT BLUE, MEDIUM BLUE FELT

WHITE CHENILLE

2 1/2" METAL HAIRPIN

KITTY

1. Glue together the 2 - 1/4" pink pom-poms to make the snout and glue snout to head.

2. Cut ears and nose from pink felt and glue in place.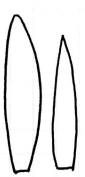

CUT 2 EARS   NOSE

3. Glue on black beads for eyes.

4. Cut cat whiskers to short lengths and glue in place under nose.

TEDDY

1. Glue 1/2" tan pom-pom to 1" tan pom-pom.

2. Glue ears to head as shown.

3. Glue eyes in place.

BUNNY

1. Glue together the 2 - 1/4" light blue pom-poms and the pink pom-pom as shown.

2. Glue assembled snout and nose to head.

3. Make teeth from a very short piece of white chenille in place under snout.

4. Cut ears from light and medium blue felt. Glue inner ear to outer ear and then glue to head.

Glue all three faces to the metal hairpin base.

VISOR FOR
PURPLE
CRITTER

FEET

FEET WITH
TOES

MATERIALS

RED

1 - 1" RED POM-POM (HEAD)

1 - 3mm PINK POM-POM (NOSE)

2 - 6mm WIGGLE EYES

YELLOW-ORANGE FELT

WOOL DOLLS HAIR

DOUBLE-SIDED TAPE

BLUE

1 - 1" ORANGE POM-POM (HEAD)

1 - 3mm PINK POM-POM (NOSE)

2 - 6mm WIGGLE EYES

YELLOW-ORANGE FELT

YELLOW-GREEN BUMP CHENILLE

DOUBLE-SIDED TAPE

PURPLE

1 - 1" PURPLE POM-POM (HEAD)

1 - 3mm PINK POM-POM (NOSE)

2 - 6mm WIGGLE EYES

RED AND WHITE FELT

DOUBLE-SIDED TAPE

GREEN

1 - 1" GREEN POM-POM (HEAD)

1 - 3mm PINK POM-POM (NOSE)

2 - 6mm WIGGLE EYES

GREEN EMBROIDERY FLOSS (HAIR)

YELLOW-ORANGE FELT

DOUBLE-SIDED TAPE

ORANGE

1 - 1" ORANGE POM-POM (HEAD)

1 - 3mm PINK POM-POM (NOSE)

2 - 6mm WIGGLE EYES

RED FELT

DOUBLE-SIDED TAPE

1. All 5 of these little critters start the same way. Glue on the eyes, nose and feet.

2. Make up your own head coverings. Use your imagination or refer to the photo and the drawings.

3. Have fun, be creative, there are no wrong ways to do this project.

4. Attach to clothing with double sided tape.

MATERIALS

1 - 1" PINK POM-POM (HEAD)

3 - 1/4" PINK POM-POMS (SNOUT & EARS)

3 - 3mm BLACK BEADS

SMALL PIECE OF LACE

1 YARD MAUVE RIBBON 1" WIDE

3" METAL HAIRPIN BASE

1. Start by making the teddy. Glue the small pink pom-poms in place for ears and snout.

2. Glue on the black beads for eyes and nose.

3. Cut a circle out of the lace and glue to back of teddy.

4. Glue one end of the ribbon to the hairpin and start making loops. Leave a little extra to stick out the side that you can trim later. Glue each loop in place and twist slightly revolving around hairpin until all ribbon is glued down. Each loop is about 2" from center.

5. Glue the assembled teddy on top of the center of the bow.

1. Glue the 2 small pink pom-poms together and then to the head.

2. Add the nose.

3. Glue eyes in place.

4. Cut inner and outer ears from white and pink felt. Glue the inner ear on top of the outer ear.

5. Cut teeth from white felt and glue in place.

6. Glue ears to head.

7. Glue assembled bunny to round wooden shape.

8. Cut 2 pieces of ribbon about 2" long each and glue to back of wood shape.

9. Glue metal pin back over ribbon.

CUT 2 EACH INNER AND OUTER EAR

TEETH

MATERIALS

1 - 1" PINK POM-POM (HEAD)

2 - 1/4" PINK POM-POMS (SNOUT)

1 - 3mm PINK POM-POM (NOSE)

2 - 3mm BLACK BEADS (EYES)

WHITE AND PINK FELT (EARS)

SHORT PIECE OF HEART RIBBON (OR ANY DECORATIVE RIBBON YOU LIKE)

1 1/4" ROUND WOOD SHAPE

SMALL METAL PIN BACK

Refrigerator Magnets

Be home
Cookies on t
table.
Love yo
Mom

Stuck-up Cat

Fat Cat

Oscar Angel

Orville Owl

Red Ted

Green Grouch

Blue Bunny

1. Glue the 2 eye pom-poms together and then glue the eyes on top of them.

2. Glue the assembly on top of the nose.

3. Glue the 3 -1" pom-poms together and then attach the assembled nose and eyes.

4. Glue the chin under the cheeks.

CUT 2
EARS

5. Cut ears from pink felt and glue on head.

6. Glue completed cat wooden base and add magnetic tape to back.

MATERIALS

3 - 1/4" PINK POM-POMS (EYES & CHIN)

1 - 1/2" PINK POM-POM (NOSE)

3 - 1" PINK POM -POMS (CHEEKS & HEAD)

2 - 5mm WIGGLE EYES

PINK FELT

1 3/4" ROUND WOOD SHAPE

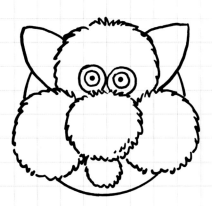

MATERIALS

1 - 2" PINK POM-POM (BODY)

2 - 3/4" PINK POM-POMS CHEEKS

1 - 1/4" RED POM-POM (NOSE)

2 - 6mm WIGGLE EYES

PURPLE EMBRIODERY FLOSS (WHISKERS)

WOODEN SPOON

2 - 7/8" POINTED OVAL WOOD SHAPES (EARS)

3/4" MAGNETIC TAPE

1 1/2" OVAL WOOD SHAPE

1. Glue together the 2 - 3/4" pink pom-poms.

2. Cut a section of bundled purple embroidery floss to about 1 1/2" length and tie in center. Glue to red pom -pom (nose).

3. Glue assembled nose and whiskers to the two 3/4" pink pom-poms.

4. Cut off the bottom of the wooden spoon leaving 2 3/4" to work with.

5. Glue the body to the bottom of the wooden spoon and then add the assembled nose, whiskers and cheeks.

6. Add a 1 1/2" oval wood shape to the back, under the ears, to make a base for the magnetic tape and then add the tape.

1. Glue nose and eyes to head.

2. Cut a small piece of brown chenille, shape it into a smile and glue under nose.

3. Glue head and arms to body.

4. Make hair from heavy yarn. Cut about 10 or 12 pieces 4" long, tie in the center and glue to top of head.

5. Cut wings from ivory felt and glue in place on back.

6. Glue body of assembled angel to round wood shape.

7. Add magnetic shape.

CUT 2 WINGS

MATERIALS

1 - 1 1/2" PINK POM-POM (BODY)

1 - 1" PINK POM-POM (HEAD)

2 - 3/4" PINK POM-POMS (ARMS)

1 - 1/4" PINK POM-POM (NOSE)

IVORY COLORED FELT (WINGS)

IVORY HEAVY YARN (HAIR)

1 3/4" ROUND WOOD SHAPE

2 - 3mm BLACK BEADS (EYES)

3/4" MAGNETIC TAPE

BROWN CHENILLE (MOUTH)

1. Cut top of head from brown felt and glue to pom-pom.

2. Make beak from a small section of orange bump chenille and glue in place.

3. Glue eyes on either side of beak.

4. Glue owl to round wood shape and add magnetic tape to back.

MATERIALS

1 - 1 1/2" TAN POM-POM (HEAD)

2 - 10 mm EYES

ORANGE BUMP CHENILLE (BEAK)

BURNT-ORANGE FELT

1 1/4" ROUND WOOD SHAPE

1/2" MAGNETIC TAPE

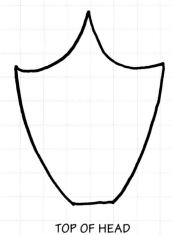

TOP OF HEAD

1. All of these small critters are very much alike. Simply glue the eyes and nose in place as shown in the drawings.

2. The bunny's ears are cut from short sections of pink bump chenille.

3. The green grouch's eyes are mounted on the 1/4" green pom-poms before attaching to head.

4. The final step is gluing to the round wood shape and adding the magnetic tape.

RED TED

GREEN GROUCH

BLUE BUNNY

MATERIALS

RED TED

1 - 1" RED POM-POM (HEAD)

1 - 1/4" PURPLE POM-POM (NOSE)

2 - 1/4" YELLOW POM-POMS (EARS)

2 - 6mm WIGGLE EYES

3/4" ROUND WOOD SHAPE (BASE)

1/2" MAGNETIC TAPE

GREEN GROUCH

1 - 3/4" MEDIUM GREEN POM-POM (HEAD)

2 - 1/4" DARK GREEN POM-POMS (EYE SUPPORTS)

1 - 3mm PINK POM-POM (NOSE)

2 - 5mm WIGGLE EYES

3/4" ROUND WOOD SHAPE (BASE)

1/2" MAGNETIC TAPE

BLUE BUNNY

1 - 3/4" LIGHT BLUE POM-POM (HEAD)

2 - 1/4" LIGHT BLUE POM-POMS (CHEEKS)

1 - 3mm PINK POM-POM (NOSE)

2 - 5mm WIGGLE EYES

LIGHT PINK BUMP CHENILLE (EARS)

3/4" ROUND WOOD SHAPE (BASE)

Holidays

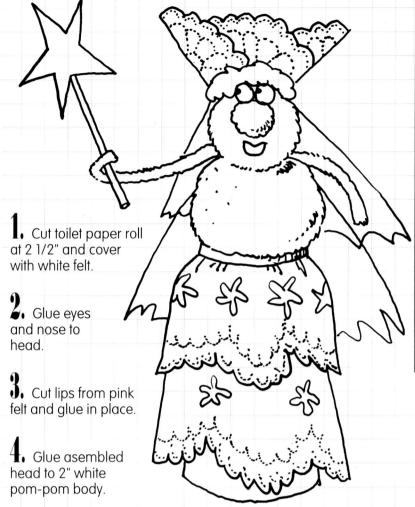

1. Cut toilet paper roll at 2 1/2" and cover with white felt.

2. Glue eyes and nose to head.

3. Cut lips from pink felt and glue in place.

4. Glue asembled head to 2" white pom-pom body.

5. Cut approximately 4" of white chenille for arms and wrap around back of head. Allow a little extra for the hand holding magic wand. Glue in place..

6. Glue assembled head and body on top of toilet paper roll.

7. Cut 10 or 12 strands of thick yarn about 5" long, and glue to top of head.

8. Cut veil and skirt from scraps of lace. Imagine how you would like it to look. Experiment, decorate to please yourself.

9. Cut star from golden yellow felt. Cut tips off of Q-Tip and glue star to one end. Glue the other end to the hand. Wrap the chenille around the Q-Tip to make the hand.

10. Cut a small pie shaped section from a paper doily for the crown. Glue to top of head over hair.

MATERIALS

1 - 2" WHITE POM-POM (BODY)

1 - 1" PINK POM POM (HEAD)

1 - 1/2" PINK POM-POM (NOSE)

2 - 5mm WIGGLE EYES

PAPER DOILY (CROWN)

TOILET PAPER ROLL

GOLDEN YELLOW, DARK PINK AND WHITE FELT

WHITE CHENILLE (ARMS)

IVORY THICK YARN (HAIR)

LACE SCRAPS (DRESS AND VEIL)

1 Q-TIP

LIPS

MATERIALS

1 - 2" TAN POM-POM (BODY)

1 - 1/2" TAN POM-POM (HEAD)

1 - 3/4" RED POM-POM (NOSE)

2 - 7mm WIGGLE EYES

BROWN WAVY HAIR

BURNT-ORANGE FELT

BURNT-ORANGE CHENILLE

BURNT-ORANGE BUMP CHENILLE

2 WOODEN CLOTHES PINS

ICE CREAM STICK

1. Glue nose and eyes to head.

2. Make antlers from burnt- orange chenille and glue to head.

3. Glue clothespins to each end of 2" tan pom-pom, and then glue head to one clothespin.

4. Glue a clump of brown wavy hair to head over antlers.

5. Cut ears from burnt-orange felt and glue to head under antlers.

6. Add one section of burnt- orange, bump chenille for tail.

7. Cut a 2 1/4" piece of ice cream or craft stick, and glue to bottom of one side of clothespin for support.

CUT 2
EARS

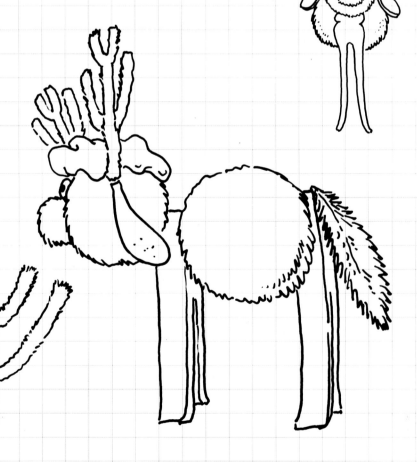

1. Cut mouth from hot pink felt and fold in half, and glue top half to one green 3/4" pom-pom and the bottom half to the other 3/4" green pom-pom as shown.

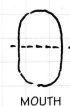

MOUTH

2. Glue eyes to blue pom-poms, and place on top of head. Add black bead for nose.

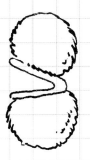

3. Twist red and white chenille to make candy cane. Bend at top to make hook. Glue to side of head.

4. Glue 1" green pom-pom to other side of candy cane.

5. Cut a small piece of candy cane, and place in mouth.

MATERIALS

CANDY CANE WORM TREE ORNAMENT

1 - 1" GREEN POM-POM (BODY)

2 - 3/4" GREEN POM-POMS (HEAD)

2- 1/4" DARK BLUE POM-POMS

HOT PINK FELT (MOUTH)

RED AND WHITE CHENILLE

1 - 3mm BLACK BEAD (NOSE)

2 - 5mm WIGGLE EYES

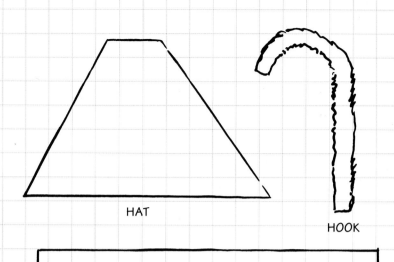

HAT

HOOK

HAT BAND

MATERIALS

1 - 2" PINK POM-POM (HEAD)

1 - 3/4" RED POM-POM (NOSE)

2 - 7mm WIGGLE EYES

RED AND WHITE FELT (HAT)

WHITE CHENILLE (HOOK)

WHITE WOOL DOLL HAIR

1. Glue eyes and nose to head.

2. Cut hat from red felt, and glue into a cone shape.

3. Cut hat band from white felt, and glue around bottom of hat.

4. Cut short length of white chenille, and bend into hook shape at top.

5. Make the beard and hair from white wool doll hair, and glue on head.

6. Glue hook inside hat, and then, glue hat to head over hair.

1. Cut a short pointed section of orange bump chenille, and glue to head.

2. Glue eyes and mouth in place.

3. Glue head to body, and add the arms.

4. Glue the assembled snowman to the round wood disk for support.

5. Add the plastic hat.

MATERIALS

1 - 2" WHITE POM-POM (BODY)

1 - 1 1/2" WHITE POM-POM (HEAD)

2 - 3/4" WHITE POM-POMS (ARMS)

3 - 3mm BLACK BEADS (EYES AND MOUTH)

ORANGE BUMP CHENILLE (NOSE)

PLASTIC TOP HAT

1 3/4" ROUND WOOL SHAPE

MATERIALS

2 - 1" GREEN POM-POMS (HEAD AND JAW)

1 - 1/4" PURPLE POM-POM (NOSE)

2 - 4.5mm CAT'S EYES

WHITE CHENILLE TEETH

BLACK CHENILLE (WING SUPPORTS)

BLACK BUMP CHENILLE HAIR

BLACK, GREEN, RED FELT (WINGS AND & EARS AND MOUTH)

1 - 1 1/4" ROUND WOOL SHAPE

1/2" MAGNETIC TAPE

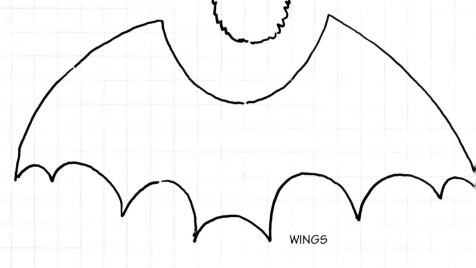

MOUTH

CUT 2 EARS

WINGS

1. Cut mouth from red felt, and fold in half.

2. Glue between the two 1" green pom-poms to create the head and jaw as shown

3. Add eyes and nose.

4. Cut ears from green felt, and glue to head.

5. Cut wings from black felt. Then, cut a 4" piece of black chenille for wing support. Curve the chenille slightly, and glue to back of wings.

6. Glue wings behind jaw.

7. Cut a short piece of black bump chenille for the pointed hair on top.

8. Glue assembled bat to round wood shape.

9. Trim a few small pieces of white chenille to fit in mouth
for teeth and fangs, and glue in place.

10. Add magnetic tape to back of wood shape, and hang on refrigerator.

GHOST

1. Glue nose and eyes to head.

2. Glue head to body.

3. Cut sheet and hood from white felt, and wrap around body and head, and glue.

4. Glue assembled ghost to round wood shape.

CUT 2: FOR SHEET AND HOOD

MATERIALS

2 - 1" WHITE POM-POM (HEAD AND BODY)

1 - 1/4" WHITE POM-POM (NOSE)

1 - 1" ORANGE POM-POM (PUMPKIN)

4 - 3mm BLACK BEADS

BLACK AND WHITE FELT

TAN CHENILLE

2 - 3/4" ROUND WOOD DISKS

PUMPKIN

1. Cut nose and mouth from black felt, and glue in place.

2. Glue eyes.

3. Cut a very short piece of tan chenille, and glue to top of head for stem.

4. Glue assembled pumpkin to round wood shape.

NOSE

MOUTH

MATERIALS

1 - 1" LIGHT GREEN POM-POM (HEAD)

2 - 3/4" LIGHT GREEN POM-POMS (JAW AND HIPS)

LIGHT GREEN AND WHITE CHENILLE

BLACK FELT

2 - 3mm BLACK BEADS

2" OVAL WOODEN SHAPE

1. cut mouth from black felt and fold in half. Glue top half to head and bottom half to jaw.

2. Cut nose from black felt and glue in place. Glue eyes on either side of nose.

3. Cut a small piece of chenille and put in mouth to make teeth.

4. Cut and bend light green chenille as shown in drawing.

5. Glue ribs and shoulders to spine.

6. Glue assembled upper body to 3/4" light green pom-pom. (hips)

7. Glue legs to hips and bottom of spine.

8. Glue assembled skeleton to oval wood shape.

9. Glue head to right arm of skeleton

note: This model is difficult to make stand. If it falls over you can add another oval wood shape. Twist and bend chenille until it is balanced.

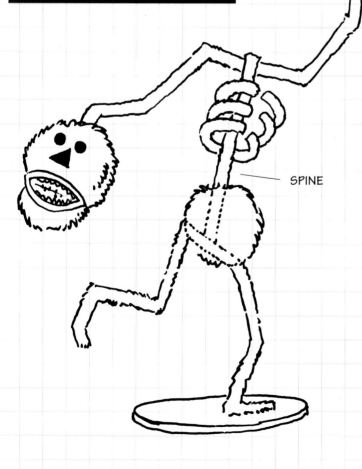

SPINE

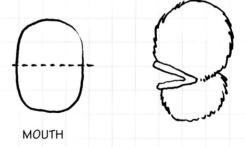

MOUTH

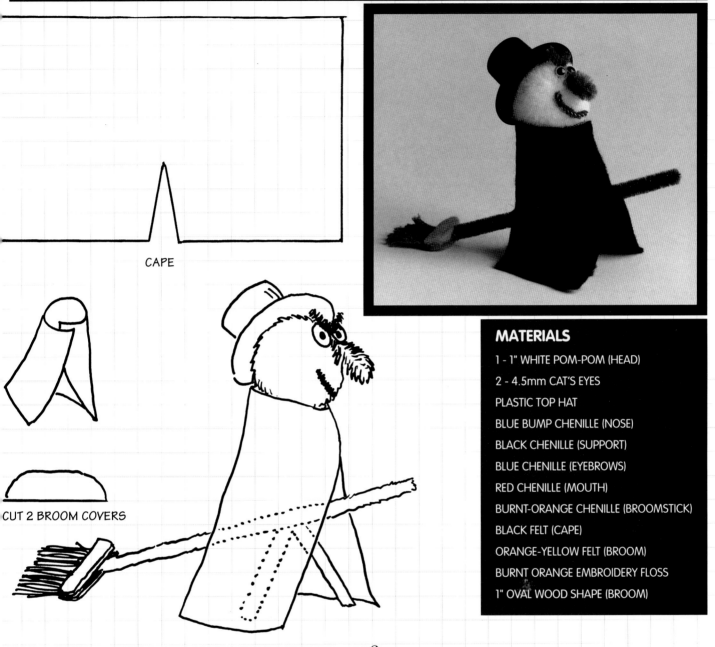

CAPE

CUT 2 BROOM COVERS

MATERIALS

1 - 1" WHITE POM-POM (HEAD)

2 - 4.5mm CAT'S EYES

PLASTIC TOP HAT

BLUE BUMP CHENILLE (NOSE)

BLACK CHENILLE (SUPPORT)

BLUE CHENILLE (EYEBROWS)

RED CHENILLE (MOUTH)

BURNT-ORANGE CHENILLE (BROOMSTICK)

BLACK FELT (CAPE)

ORANGE-YELLOW FELT (BROOM)

BURNT ORANGE EMBROIDERY FLOSS

1" OVAL WOOD SHAPE (BROOM)

1. Cut a short piece of blue bump chenille for nose and glue to head.

2. Glue eyes over nose

3. Make eyebrows from blue chenille, and glue over eyes.

4. Cut a small piece of red chenille, and trim off almost all the fuzzy. Then, make a smile and glue under nose.

5. Cut the cape from black felt, and glue the ends together at the top. Glue under head. (measure size of top of cape to match size of head before gluing.)

6. Glue on the top hat.

7. Cut the broom covers from orange-yellow felt.

8. Cut a bunch of embroidery to about one inch and glue to the oval wood shape. Glue the two broom covers over the wood shape.

9. Glue the broom to the handle, and then glue the handle to the openings in the cape.

10. Cut a section of black chenille about 2" long and bend in half. Glue inside cape to bottom of broom handle for support.

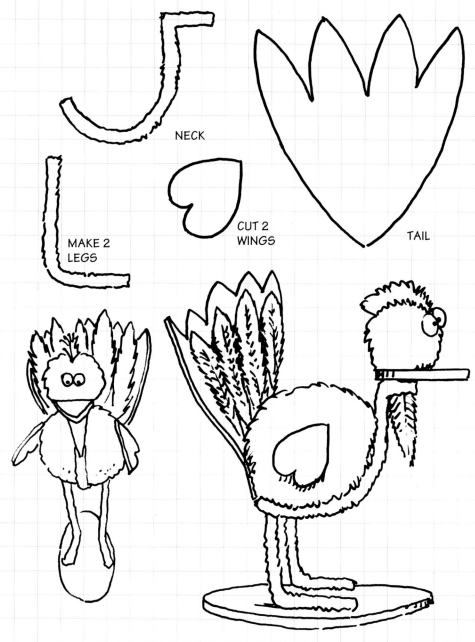

NECK

CUT 2 WINGS

TAIL

MAKE 2 LEGS

MATERIALS

1 - 1 1/2" MEDIUM BLUE POM-POM (BODY)

1- 3/4" PURPLE POM-POM (HEAD)

YELLOW AND MEDIUM BLUE CHENILLE

2 - 5mm WIGGLE EYES

LAVENDER FELT (WINGS)

HOT PINK FELT (TAIL)

BROWN, BLUE, RED, YELLOW BUMP CHENILLE

2" OVAL WOOD SHAPE (STAND)

1" POINTED OVAL WOOD SHAPE (BEAK)

1. Glue eyes to head.

2. Glue beak to bottom of head.

3. Make crown from a small piece of red bump chenille.

4. Cut off a piece of medium blue chenille and bend as shown for neck and beak support. Glue to body.

5. Glue assembled beak and head to neck.

6. Cut wings from lavender felt and glue to side of body.

7. Cut a short piece of red bump chenille for gullet. Glue under beak on neck.

8. Make legs from yellow chenille and glue to body. Then, glue assembled bird to large oval wood shape.

9. Cut one section each of brown, blue, red and yellow bump chenille. Glue in a fan shape to back of body.

10. Cut tail from hot pink felt, and glue behind bump chenille.

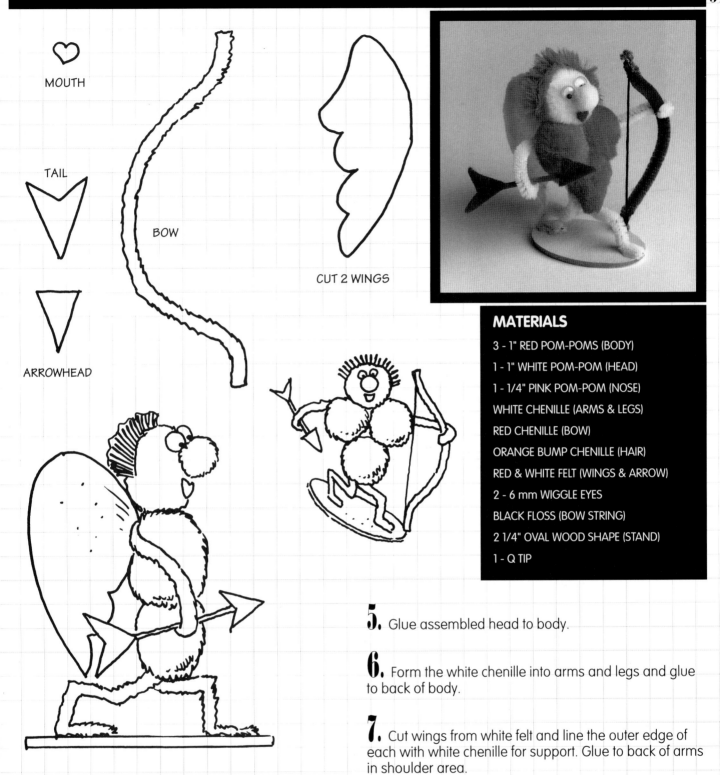

MOUTH

TAIL

ARROWHEAD

BOW

CUT 2 WINGS

MATERIALS

3 - 1" RED POM-POMS (BODY)

1 - 1" WHITE POM-POM (HEAD)

1 - 1/4" PINK POM-POM (NOSE)

WHITE CHENILLE (ARMS & LEGS)

RED CHENILLE (BOW)

ORANGE BUMP CHENILLE (HAIR)

RED & WHITE FELT (WINGS & ARROW)

2 - 6 mm WIGGLE EYES

BLACK FLOSS (BOW STRING)

2 1/4" OVAL WOOD SHAPE (STAND)

1 - Q TIP

1. Glue together the 3 red pom-poms and trim them to make a heart shape.

2. Glue nose to head. Then, glue eyes above nose.

3. Cut a section of orange bump chenille for hair and glue in place.

5. Glue assembled head to body.

6. Form the white chenille into arms and legs and glue to back of body.

7. Cut wings from white felt and line the outer edge of each with white chenille for support. Glue to back of arms in shoulder area.

8. Make bow from red chenille and string with black thread or embroidery floss.

9. Cut the ends off a Q-tip, paint it red with a marker and add the arrowhead and tail.

10. Mount assembled cupid on oval wood shape.

MATERIALS

1 - 2" PINK POM-POM (BODY)

1 - 1" PINK POM-POM (HEAD)

1 - 1/4" RED POM-POM (CHEEKS)

2 - 5 mm WIGGLE EYES

WHITE AND LIGHT GREEN FELT

DARK PINK FELT

PINK CHENILLE

ORANGE BUMP CHENILLE

1 3/4" ROUND WOOD SHAPE

1. Glue the two 1/2" pink pom-poms together, and then glue the nose between them as shown.

2. Cut teeth from white felt and glue under cheeks.
TEETH

3. Glue that assembly to 1" pink pom-pom and add the eyes.

4. Glue assembled head to 2" pink pom-pom.

5. Make arms from short pieces of pink chenille and glue to sides where the head meets the body.

6. Cut outer ears from white felt, inner ears from dark pink felt and glue together. Pinch bottoms and glue to each side of head.

7. Make carrot from a 2" length of pink bump chenille and carrot top from light green felt. Glue to carrot.

8. Place assembled carrot in right hand of bunny and glue in place.

9. Glue entire assembly to round wood shape.

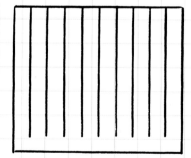
CARROT GREEN: CUT ON LINES

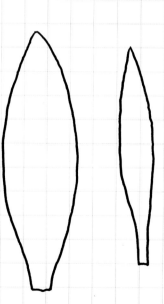
OUTER EAR   INNER EAR
CUT 2 EACH

1. Glue together the two 1/4" pink pom-poms and the 5mm pink pom-pom and glue to body.

2. Glue eyes on either side of nose.

3. Cut ears from dark and light pink felt and glue inner ears on outer ears. Then pinch together the bottoms and glue for shape.

4. Glue assembled ears to top of head as shown.

5. Glue white 1/4" pom-pom to back side for cotton tail.

6. Place in basket.

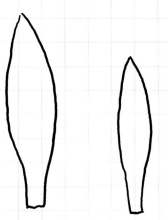

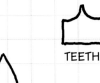

TEETH

OUTER EAR   INNER EAR
CUT 2 EACH

MATERIALS

1 - 2" PINK POM-POM (BODY)

2 - 1/4" PINK POM-POMS (SNOUT)

1 - 1/4" WHITE POM-POM (TAIL)

1 - 5 mm PINK POM-POM (NOSE)

2 - 5 mm WIGGLE EYES

WHITE, DARK PINK AND LIGHT PINK FELT

1 SMALL CRAFT BASKET

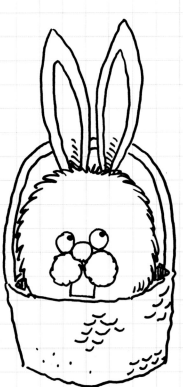

Collectables

Royal Palace Guard

Willie Worm

Tippy Troll

Betty Bookworm

Jump-up Jack

Country Girl

Reader Rabbit

Bossie

Leo The Lovable

1. Trim 2" black pom-pom until it resembles the shape of the hat.

2. Paint clothespin red below round top down to opening where it splits. Paint it black from there down. Paint the doll stand black (Use colored markers or any paint you have.)

3. Paint white dots for buttons.

4. Glue hat to top of head.

5. Glue 5mm pink pom-pom on head right up under hat.

6. Glue a piece of white chenille around clothespin about "waist high".

7. Cut 2 pieces of red chenille and glue to sides for arms. Add the 2 remaining pink pom-poms for hands.

8. Cut 2 small squares of yellow-orange felt for shoulder epaulets and glue in place.

9. Cut a short piece of black chenille or yarn for the hat strap. Glue to hat and under chin.

10. Place assembled guard in doll stand and make the gun from a wood pick or of 2 toothpicks. Glue in place.

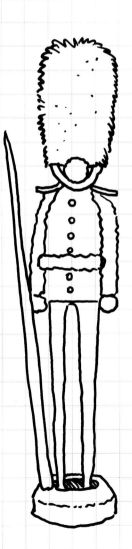

MATERIALS

1 - 2" BLACK POM-POM (HAT)

1 - ROUND WOODEN CLOTHES PIN (BODY)

1 - DOLL STAND

3 - 5 mm PINK POM-POMS (NOSE & HANDS)

WHITE, BLACK, RED CHENILLE

YELLOW-ORANGE FELT

1 - WOODEN PICK (GUN) OR 2 TOOTHPICKS

RED & BLACK MARKERS

WHITE PAINT (BUTTONS)

MATERIALS

2 - 1" LIGHT GREEN POM-POMS

2 - 3/4" BLUE POM-POMS

2 - 3/4" LIGHT GREEN POM-POMS

3 - 1/4" LIGHT GREEN POM-POMS

2 - 5 mm WIGGLE EYES

RED FELT

GREEN BUMP CHENILLE

WOODEN SPOON

1. Glue together 2-1/4" light green pom-poms and add the eyes.

2. Cut mouth from red felt, fold in half, and glue top half to 1" light green pom-pom and bottom half to other 1" light green pom-pom.

3. Glue assembled eyes to top of head and add 1/4" light green pom-pom for nose.

4. Cut one section of green bump chenille and glue to head behind eyes.

5. Glue assembld head to front of wooden spoon and add alternating blue and green 3/4" pom-poms to complete body.

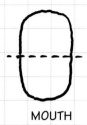

MOUTH

1. Glue together the 2" pink pom-poms.

2. Glue the nose on the head.

3. Cut ears from light pink felt and hands & feet from dark pink felt and glue to body as shown.

4. Cut a hunk of wool doll hair about 3 1/2" X 3 1/2" and glue to top of head.

5. Glue eyes in place over nose and partly over hair if the hair comes down low enough on the face.

6. Glue assembled troll to 1" round wood shape for support.

MATERIALS

2 - 2" PINK POM-POMS (BODY & HEAD)

1 - 3/4" PINK POM-POM (NOSE)

2 - 10 mm WIGGLE EYES

LIGHT & DARK PINK FELT

LIGHT CREAM COLOR WOOL DOLL HAIR

1" ROUND WOOD SHAPE

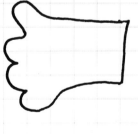

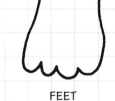

HANDS   FEET   EARS
          CUT 2 EACH

MATERIALS

2 - 1/4" BLACK POM-POMS (FACE)

1 - 1/4" RED POM-POM (NOSE)

2 - 6 mm WIGGLE EYES

BROWN AND TAN CHENILLE

1. Twist the 2 pieces of chenille together. Coil them around something round in three loops (like a spring).

2. Bend the top about 3/4" so it makes a flat place for the face and nose.

3. Glue the pom-pom on for the face and nose and then add the eyes.

1. Cut a section of toilet paper roll 2" long and cover with chartreuse felt.

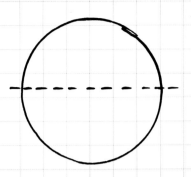

2. Cut mouth from hot pink felt. Fold in half. Glue top half to one 2" pink pom-pom and glue the bottom half to the other 2" pink pom-pom and glue the pom-poms together as shown.

MOUTH

3. Glue the 2 3/4" pink pom-poms together for upper face.

4. Glue the red nose in place over the mouth and then add the assembled upper face.

5. Glue eyes in place over nose.

6. Cut some short pieces of white chenille and glue in mouth for teeth.

7. Cut about 2 pieces of heavy black yarn. Tie together at center and glue to top of head.

8. Stuff entire character about half way down into covered toilet paper roll.

MATERIALS

2 - 2" PINK POM-POMS (HEAD & BODY)

1 - 1" RED POM-POM (NOSE)

2 - 3/4" PINK POM-POMS (UPPER FACE)

HOT PINK FELT (MOUTH)

CHARTRUESE FELT

WHITE CHENILLE (TEETH)

2 - 7 mm WIGGLE EYES

HEAVY BLACK YARN

TOILET PAPER ROLL

MATERIALS

1 - 2" PINK POM-POM (FACE)

1 - 3/4" PINK POM-POM (NOSE)

2 - 7 mm WIGGLE EYES

HOT PINK CHENILLE (MOUTH)

HOT PINK EMBROIDERY FLOSS

CREAM COLOR WOOD DOLL HAIR

SMALL STRAW HAT

CALICO RIBBON

LACE SCRAPS

TOILET PAPER ROLL

1. Cut toilet paper roll to about 2 1/2" and cover with calico ribbon or material.

2. Glue nose to center of face.

3. Glue eyes over nose.

4. Cut a short piece of hot pink chenille, curve into a smile and glue under nose.

5. Glue assembled head into top of covered toilet paper roll.

6. Cut a pretty large hunk of wool doll hair, about 7" X 4" and glue to top of head covering the back of the head too.

7. When hair is dry tie it into pony tails with hot pink embroedery floss.

8. Glue the straw hat on the head.

9. Make the skirt from lace ribbon about 1 1/2" wide or any lace scraps you may have. Wrap around body and glue in place.

1. Paint clothespins white and glue together as shown.

2. Glue white pom-poms in place as shown.

3. Glue on pink pom-pom for nose at bottom of top clothespin. Glue eyes over nose.

4. Glue assembled body to oval wood base.

5. Shape a full length of white chenille into arms and hands and glue to back of bottom clothespin just above the pom-pom.

6. Make book from any white stiff paper you have (postcard thickness is good) cut to approximately 3" X 1 3/4" and cover with red felt.

7. Fold book at center and glue to hands.

MATERIALS

2 - 1 1/2" WHITE POM-POMS (BODY)

2 - 3/4" WHITE POM-POMS (FACE &TAIL)

1 - 1/4" PINK POM-POM (NOSE)

2 - 6 mm WIGGLE EYES

2 SMALL WOODEN CLOTHESPINS

WHITE CHENILLE (ARMS)

1 - 2 1/4" OVAL WOOD SHAPE (BASE)

RED FELT FOR BOOK COVER

WHITE ACRYLIC PAINT

MATERIALS

1 - 2" WHITE POM-POM (HEAD)

1 - 1 1/2" WHITE POM-POM (BODY)

1 - 1 1/2" BLACK POM-POM (BODY)

1 - 1" PINK POM-POM (UDDER)

1 - 1/4" BLACK POM POM (TAIL)

5 - 5 mm PINK POM-POMS (UDDER)

2 - 10 mm WIGGLE EYES

BLACK & WHITE FELT

TAN AND WHITE CHENILLE

BLACK BUMP CHENILLE

2 ICE CREAM OR CRAFT STICKS (LEGS)

TOILET PAPER ROLL

BLACK THREAD

1. Cut off a 2" long piece of toilet paper roll and cover with white felt.

2. Trim fuzz off of the 2" white pom-pom to make the shape for the cows head as shown.

3. Cut nose from black felt and glue in place.

4. Glue eyes in place and cut and trim short piece of black chenille for eyelashes and glue over eyes.

5. Make mouth from a short piece of black floss or thread.

6. Cut ears from black felt, pinch ends together and glue to side of head.

7. Shape half a stick of tan chenille into horns and glue on top of head.

8. Cut a short piece of black bump chenille and glue over horns on top of head.

9. Glue completed head to 1 1/2" black pom-pom for lower neck.

10. Cut the 2 ice cream sticks in half and glue in position as legs on the covered toilet paper roll. Paint the hooves with a black marker.

11. Make the udder from a 1" pink pom-pom and the 5 mm pink pom-poms. Glue together and to underside of cow's body.

12. Insert the assembled head and neck into the front hole in the front end of toilet paper roll and glue.

13. Put the white 1 1/2" pom-pom in the back opening and glue.

14. Make a tail from white chenille and 1/4" black pom-pom. Glue in place.

15. Cut assorted shapes and sizes from black felt for the cows markings. Glue felt shapes over the ends of the craft sticks to hide the seams.

NOSE

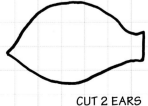

CUT 2 EARS

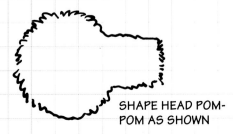

SHAPE HEAD POM-POM AS SHOWN

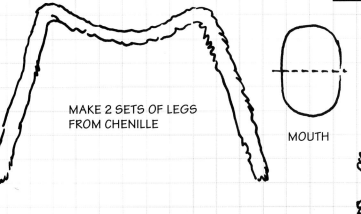

MAKE 2 SETS OF LEGS
FROM CHENILLE

MOUTH

CUT 2
EARS

MATERIALS

1 - 2" TAN POM-POM (HEAD)

2 - 3/4" TAN POM-POMS (SNOUT)

1 - 1/4" BLACK POM-POM (NOSE)

CAT WHISKERS

2 - 6mm WIGGLE EYES

RED AND OCHRE FELT

BROWN AND WHITE CHENILLE

RUST COLORED BUMP CHENILLE

CREAM COLORED WOOL DOLL HAIR (MANE)

TOILET PAPER ROLL

1. Cut a 2 3/4" long section of toilet paper roll and cover with ochre colored felt.

2. Cut mouth from red felt and fold in half. Glue top half to
3/4" tan pom-pom. Glue bottom half to the other 3/4" tan pom-pom as shown.

3. Glue finished section to center of 2" tan pom-pom.

4. Glue nose in place. Make teeth from a short section of white chenille.

5. Cut ears from yellow ochre felt and glue to sides of head. Then, Glue eyes in place.

6. Take a big bunch of wool doll hair and glue all around head to make a fuzzy mane.

7. Cut 8 pieces 1 1/2" long of cat whiskers and glue under nose..

8. Make legs from 2 pieces 7" long of brown chenille and glue to body.

9. Cut a circle the size of the opening in the toilet paper roll from the yellow ochre felt to cover the back side of the body and glue.

10. Cut a section of bump chenille and glue in place for tail.

11. Glue assembled lions head with mane into place in front opening of toilet paper roll.

Birds

CUT 2 WINGS

TAIL

MATERIALS

2 - 2 " LAVENDER POM-POMS (HEAD & BODY)

2 - 10mm WIGGLE EYES

HOT PINK FELT (WINGS & TAILS)

RED & YELLOW BUMP CHENILLE

2 - 1 1/2" POINTED OVAL WOOD SHAPES

HOT PINK EMBROIDERY FLOSS

1. Cut a section fo red bump chenille for the beak and glue to 2" lavender pom-pom. Glue eyes on either side as shown.

2. Cut a bunch of strands about 2" long from the hot pink embroidery floss. Glue together at one end and glue to back of head.

3. Cut wings and tail from hot pink felt and glue to top of second lavender pom-pom.

4. Glue assembled head on body on top of wings and tail.

5. Make legs from 2 sections of yellow bump chenille and glue to body. Bend legs at bottom and glue to pointed oval wood shapes for feet. If you need additional support to make it stand, glue to an oval wood shape.

1. Cut a very short pointed piece of yellow bump chenille and glue to center of black pom-pom for beak. Glue eyes above beak.

2. Cut about 10 strands 2" long of black yarn, tie together at center and glue to top of head.

3. Glue assembled head to white pom-pom.

4. Cut cape and bow tie from black felt and glue on body.

5. Cut feet from yellow-orange felt and glue in place.

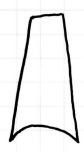

CUT 2 FEET

BOW TIE

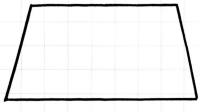

CAPE

MATERIALS

1 - 1" BLACK POM-POM (HEAD)

1 - 1" WHITE POM-POM (BODY)

2 - 5mm WIGGLE EYES

BLACK AND YELLOW-ORANGE FELT

HEAVY BLACK YARN

YELLOW BUMP CHENILLE (BEAK)

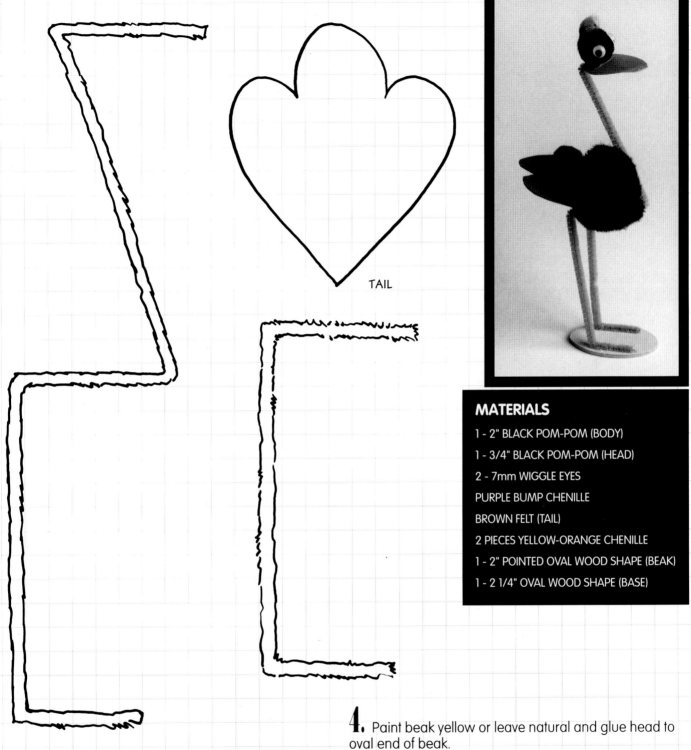

TAIL

MATERIALS

1 - 2" BLACK POM-POM (BODY)

1 - 3/4" BLACK POM-POM (HEAD)

2 - 7mm WIGGLE EYES

PURPLE BUMP CHENILLE

BROWN FELT (TAIL)

2 PIECES YELLOW-ORANGE CHENILLE

1 - 2" POINTED OVAL WOOD SHAPE (BEAK)

1 - 2 1/4" OVAL WOOD SHAPE (BASE)

1. Take a full piece of yellow-orange chenille and bend for foot, leg, neck and beak support as shown.

2. Cut second chenille to 6"and bend as shown for second leg.

3. Glue eyes to head and cut a short piece of purple bump chenille for crown and glue in place.

4. Paint beak yellow or leave natural and glue head to oval end of beak.

5. Cut tail from brown felt and glue to 2" black pom-pom.

6. Glue head and beak to top bend in long leg and glue body and tail at the bend in the middle of same leg.

7. Glue second leg in place under body and glue both legs to the oval wood shape.

1. Cut bill from yellow-orange felt and fold in half. Glue top half to head and bottom half to body as shown.

2. Glue beads on head over beak.

3. Cut a short piece of orange bump chenille and glue on top of head for crown.

4. Cut feet from yellow-orange felt and glue to bottom of body.

5. Glue assembled bird on top of wood shape for support.

MATERIALS

1 - 1 1/2" WHITE POM-POM (BODY)

1 - 3/4" YELLOW POM-POM (HEAD)

2 - 3mm BLACK BEADS (EYES)

ORANGE BUMP CHENILLE (CROWN)

ORANGE AND YELLOW-ORANGE FELT

1 - 1 1/4" ROUND WOOD SHAPE

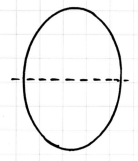

BILL

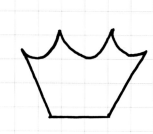

FEET

1. Glue the eyes to the top of the oval wood shape.

2. Cut a bunch of hot pink embroidery floss to about 1 1/2" lengths. The easiest way to keep it together is to cut it all at once by cutting through part of the wrapper. Glue it to the back of the wood shape.

3. Glue completed section on top of the green pom-pom.

4. Cut a whole bunch of the heavy yarn and glue it on top of the doll stand to make a nest.

5. Glue the assembled bird into the nest.

MATERIALS

1 - 1" GREEN POM-POM

2 - 6mm WIGGLE EYES

1 - 1 1/2" POINTED OVAL WOOD SHAPE

HOT PINK EMBROIDERY FLOSS

CREAM HEAVY YARN

DOLL STAND

1. Glue small yellow pom-pom on top of large one.

2. Cut the point off of one toothpick at about 1 1/2" and glue to head for beak.

3. Glue eyes directly above beak.

4. Cut a short piece of orange bump chenille and glue on top of head to make a crown.

5. Cut the pointed ends off of the other two toothpicks. Glue to body at one end and round wood shape at other.

MATERIALS

1 - 1 1/2" YELLOW POM-POM
1 - 3/4" YELLOW POM-POM
ORANGE BUMP CHENILLE
2 - 5 mm WIGGLE EYES
3 TOOTHPICKS
1 3/4" ROUND WOOD SHAPE

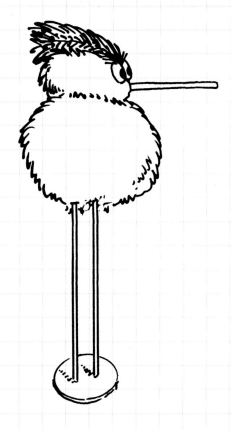

1. Paint pointed oval wood shape yellow with marker or acrylic paint. Glue on eyes.

2. Cut a bunch of hot pink embroidery floss to 1 1/2" and tie together at center so the bunch is shaped as shown.

3. Glue floss to back of head.

4. Glue completed head to black pom-pom.

5. Cut the points off the toothpicks and glue to body and base.

MATERIALS

1 - 1" BLACK POM-POM

2 - 6mm WIGGLE EYES

2 - TOOTHPICKS

HOT PINK EMBROIDERY FLOSS

1 - 1 1/1" WOOD OVAL POINTED SHAPE

1 - 3/4" ROUND WOOD SHAPE

— 2 1/4" —
CUT 2 LEGS FROM
YELLOW CHENILLE

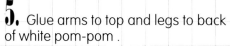

— 3" FOR ARMS —

MATERIALS

1 - 2" WHITE POM-POM (BODY)

1 - 1 1/2" YELLOW POM-POM (HEAD)

1 - 3/4" WHITE POM-POM (TAIL)

2 - 5mm WIGGLE EYES

ORANGE BUMP CHENILLE (BEAK)

YELLOW CHENILLE (ARMS & LEGS)

CREAM HEAVY YARN

BLACK AND YELLOW-ORANGE FELT

PAPER ABOUT THE WEIGHT OF A POST CARD

PHOTO OF A FRIEND

1. Cut a piece of card stock 2 1/8" X 5" and pieces of black and yellow orange felt the same size. Glue felt to front and back of cut card and fold at center, black inside.

2. Cut a section of orange bump chenille and glue to head for beak. Glue eyes on head over beak.

3. Cut about 15 pieces 3 1/2" long of heavy cream colored yarn. Tie at center and glue on top of head.

4. Make arms and legs from yellow chenille to sizes shown in drawing.

5. Glue arms to top and legs to back of white pom-pom .

6. Place assembled body inside folded covered card as shown and glue.

7. Glue completed head on top of folded card.

8. Glue a small picture on front and bend arms in position as shown.

9. Glue tail on back.